PITTSBURGH STEELERS
ALL-TIME GREATS

BY TED COLEMAN

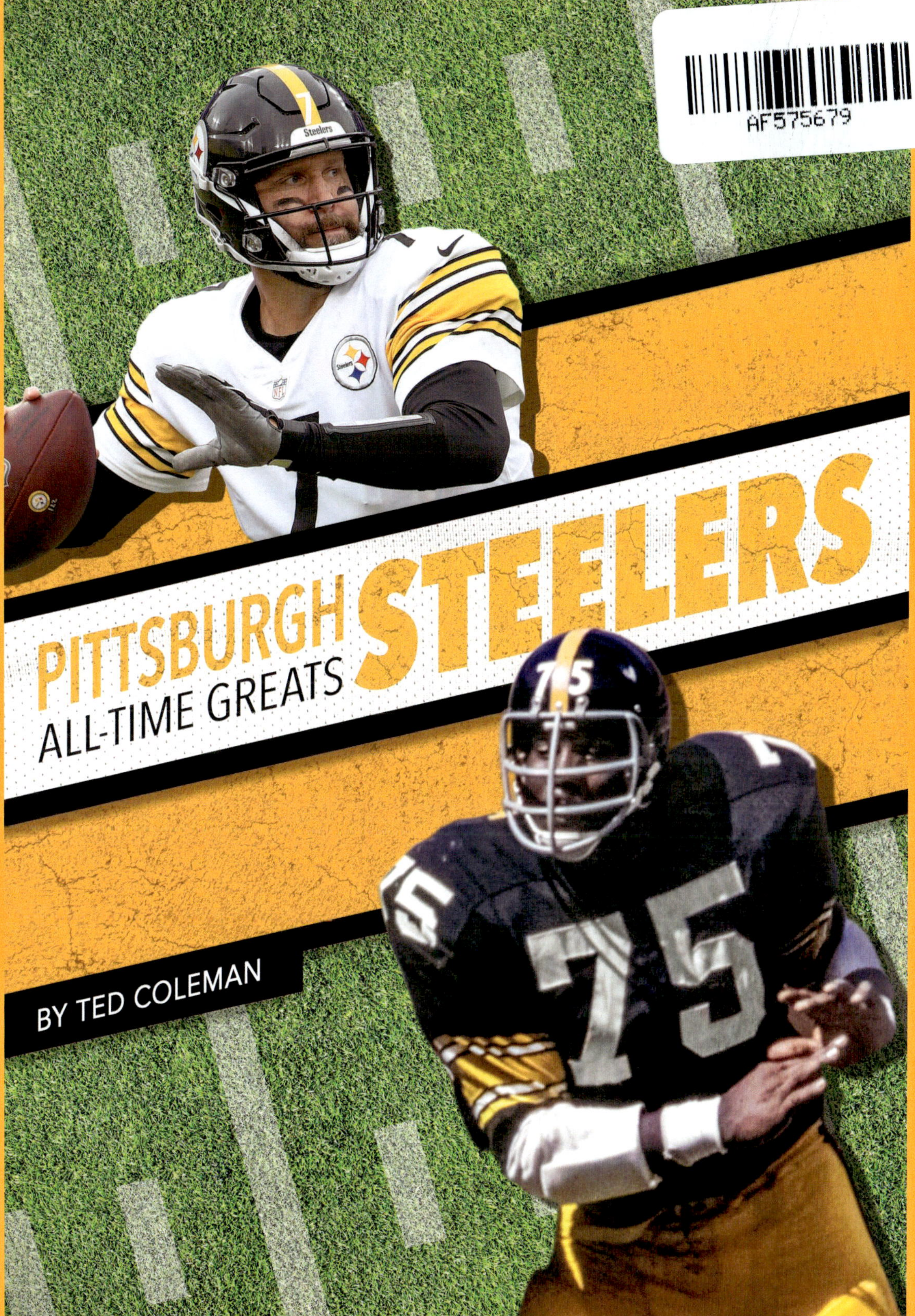

Book design by Jake Slavik
Cover design by Jake Slavik

Photographs ©: Nick Wass/AP Images, cover (top), 1 (top); Tony Tomsic/AP Images, cover (bottom), 1 (bottom), 9; Peter Read Miller/AP Images, 4; Harry Cabluck/AP Images, 7; Vernon Biever/AP Images, 10; David Durochik/AP Images, 13; Al Messerschmidt/AP Images, 14; Jim Mahoney/AP Images, 16; Amy Sancetta/AP Images, 19; Mark Zaleski/AP Images, 21

Press Box Books, an imprint of Press Room Editions.

ISBN
978-1-63494-364-2 (library bound)
978-1-63494-381-9 (paperback)
978-1-63494-414-4 (epub)
978-1-63494-398-7 (hosted ebook)

Library of Congress Control Number: 2020952637

Distributed by North Star Editions, Inc.
2297 Waters Drive
Mendota Heights, MN 55120
www.northstareditions.com

Printed in the United States of America
082021

ABOUT THE AUTHOR

Ted Coleman is a sportswriter who lives in Louisville, Kentucky, with his trusty Affenpinscher, Chloe.

TABLE OF CONTENTS

BRADSHAW
12

CHAPTER 1
A WINNING OFFENSE

The Pittsburgh Steelers were founded in 1933. They are one of the oldest teams in the National Football League (NFL). But for their first few decades, the Steelers didn't have much success. That changed in the 1970s. Several legendary players made the Steelers truly great.

In 1970, Pittsburgh used the top draft pick to choose quarterback **Terry Bradshaw**. Bradshaw took a lot of risks and threw a lot of interceptions. But he also had one of the league's strongest arms. He earned Most Valuable Player (MVP) honors in 1978. More importantly, Bradshaw led his team to four

Super Bowl victories. In two of them, he was the game's MVP.

Bradshaw didn't do it alone. The Steelers were loaded with offensive talent. Running back **Franco Harris** was a big, powerful runner. He also had great hands. In a 1972 playoff game, Harris made a miracle catch off a deflected pass. The catch became known as the "Immaculate Reception." It helped Pittsburgh win its first playoff game.

Bradshaw's main receiving target was **Lynn Swann**. Swann stood only 5-foot-11. But he made up for it with speed and jumping ability.

STAT SPOTLIGHT

CAREER RUSHING YARDS

STEELERS TEAM RECORD

Franco Harris: 11,950

In the 1975 season, his soaring catch in the Super Bowl helped win him the game's MVP award. He was the first receiver to win it.

Swann's receiving partner for many years was John Stallworth. Stallworth was tall but still fast. Injuries slowed him down. But Stallworth battled through. In the 1979 season, he caught the game-winning touchdown in the Super Bowl. When Stallworth retired after the 1987 season, he held the team record for career receiving yards.

Snapping the ball to Bradshaw was center Mike Webster. Webster became known for his toughness,

OUTSTANDING O-LINE

Pittsburgh's top offensive players were aided by a great line of blockers. After Webster, Dermontti Dawson played a Hall of Fame career at center from 1988 to 2000. Alan Faneca was another Hall of Famer. The guard made seven Pro Bowls as a Steeler. In the modern era, David DeCastro and Maurkice Pouncey were also regular Pro Bowlers.

earning the name "Iron Mike." He often played with no sleeves, even in cold weather. His toughness inspired his teammates. They chose Webster as a team captain nine times.

GREENE
75

CHAPTER 2

THE STEEL CURTAIN

The Steelers' offensive weapons won them plenty of games. But the 1970s teams were built on defense. Pittsburgh's defense earned a reputation for toughness. People called them the "Steel Curtain." The centerpiece was defensive tackle **"Mean" Joe Greene**. Greene made his name as one of the most fearsome players in NFL history. Big, strong, and fast, Greene set the tone for the defense.

In the secondary was cornerback **Mel Blount**. Rules of the day meant cornerbacks could play receivers much tougher. Blount hit big and often separated the ball from his opponents. Quarterbacks feared throwing his way.

Linebacker **Jack Ham** mostly played before sacks were an official statistic. But Ham definitely racked up plenty of them. He was a smart player with great instincts. In 1975, Ham was named Defensive Player of the Year.

Ham's fellow linebacker **Jack Lambert** was missing teeth from a high school basketball injury. To intimidate opponents, Lambert chose not to wear his false teeth during games. Lambert scared opponents with his playing style, too. He made nine Pro Bowls during his

STAT SPOTLIGHT

CAREER INTERCEPTIONS

STEELERS TEAM RECORD

Mel Blount: 57

HAM
59

career. He was also the 1976 Defensive Player of the Year.

From 1974 to 1987, Steelers fans could count on one thing. **Donnie Shell** would intercept at least one pass every year. Shell finished with 51 interceptions during his 14-year career. At the time, that was the most ever for a strong safety. Shell was also a big hitter, and he made a lot of tackles. He led the secondary in tackles six years in a row.

L. C. Greenwood wasn't as famous as Joe Greene. But he was just as mean. Greenwood flew off the end of the defensive line. He used a blend of speed and strength to get to the quarterback. These players made the Steel Curtain one of the greatest defenses in NFL history.

COACHING STABILITY

Between 1969 and 2021, the Steelers had just three head coaches. **Chuck Noll** was Pittsburgh's head coach in 1969 through the 1991 season. Then **Bill Cowher** led the Steelers from 1992 to 2006. **Mike Tomlin** took over in 2007 and was still going strong in 2021. Each coach did a lot of winning. All three won at least one Super Bowl.

ROETHLISBERGER
7

CHAPTER 3
MORE SUPER BOWLS

The Steel Curtain era ended in the 1980s. But Pittsburgh maintained a solid defense. Cornerback **Rod Woodson** began his Hall of Fame career in Pittsburgh. He was an excellent athlete who also returned kicks and punts.

Jerome Bettis was a big running back like Franco Harris. But Bettis used his bruising style to run people over. His toughness made him great at scoring from the goal line. Bettis retired on a high note after the 2005 season. He helped the Steelers win their fifth Super Bowl.

Quarterback **Ben Roethlisberger** led that 2005 team. He was a big quarterback but also very mobile. Roethlisberger rewrote the Steelers' record book. In 2017, he became just the eighth quarterback in NFL history to top 50,000 passing yards.

Roethlisberger's favorite target was **Hines Ward**. Ward had excellent hands and was a great blocker. In the 2005 season, Ward was the MVP of the Super Bowl. In that game, he had 123 receiving yards and a touchdown.

And of course, the Steelers had a great defense. Fans often saw safety **Troy Polamalu** sprinting across the field to make a tackle. His long black hair flowed behind

STAT SPOTLIGHT

CAREER RECEIVING YARDS

STEELERS TEAM RECORD

Hines Ward: 12,083

WARD
86

him like a cape.

Linebacker **James Harrison** was the team's best pass rusher. He earned Defensive Player of the Year honors in 2008. Best of all, Harrison helped the Steelers win another Super Bowl that season.

SANTONIO HOLMES

Santonio Holmes played only four seasons in Pittsburgh. But he made one of the greatest catches in Super Bowl history. In the Super Bowl after the 2008 season, Pittsburgh trailed late in the fourth quarter. Then Holmes caught a 6-yard touchdown pass, barely keeping his toes in the end zone. The Steelers took the lead with just 35 seconds left and won the game.

Wide receivers **Antonio Brown** and **JuJu Smith-Schuster** continued Ward's legacy. The flashy and exciting Brown racked up more than 11,000 yards as a Steeler from 2010 to 2018. Then Smith-Schuster took

over as the team's top receiver. The speedster notched more than 3,700 yards in his first four seasons. Steelers fans hoped for many more legends and another Super Bowl ring.

TIMELINE

1969
1970
1980
1990
2000
2010
2020
L. C. GREENWOOD
(1969–81)
TERRY BRADSHAW
(1970–83)
FRANCO HARRIS
(1972–83)
JACK LAMBERT
(1974–84)
JOHN STALLWORTH
(1974–87)
ROD WOODSON
(1987–96)
HINES WARD
(1998–2011)
TROY POLAMALU
(2003–14)
ANTONIO BROWN
(2010–18)
JOE GREENE
(1969–81)
MEL BLOUNT
(1970–83)
JACK HAM
(1971–82)
LYNN SWANN
(1974–82)
DONNIE SHELL
(1974–87)
MIKE WEBSTER
(1974–88)
JEROME BETTIS
(1996–2005)
JAMES HARRISON
(2002, 2004–12, 2014–17)
BEN ROETHLISBERGER
(2004–)
JUJU SMITH-SCHUSTER
(2017–)

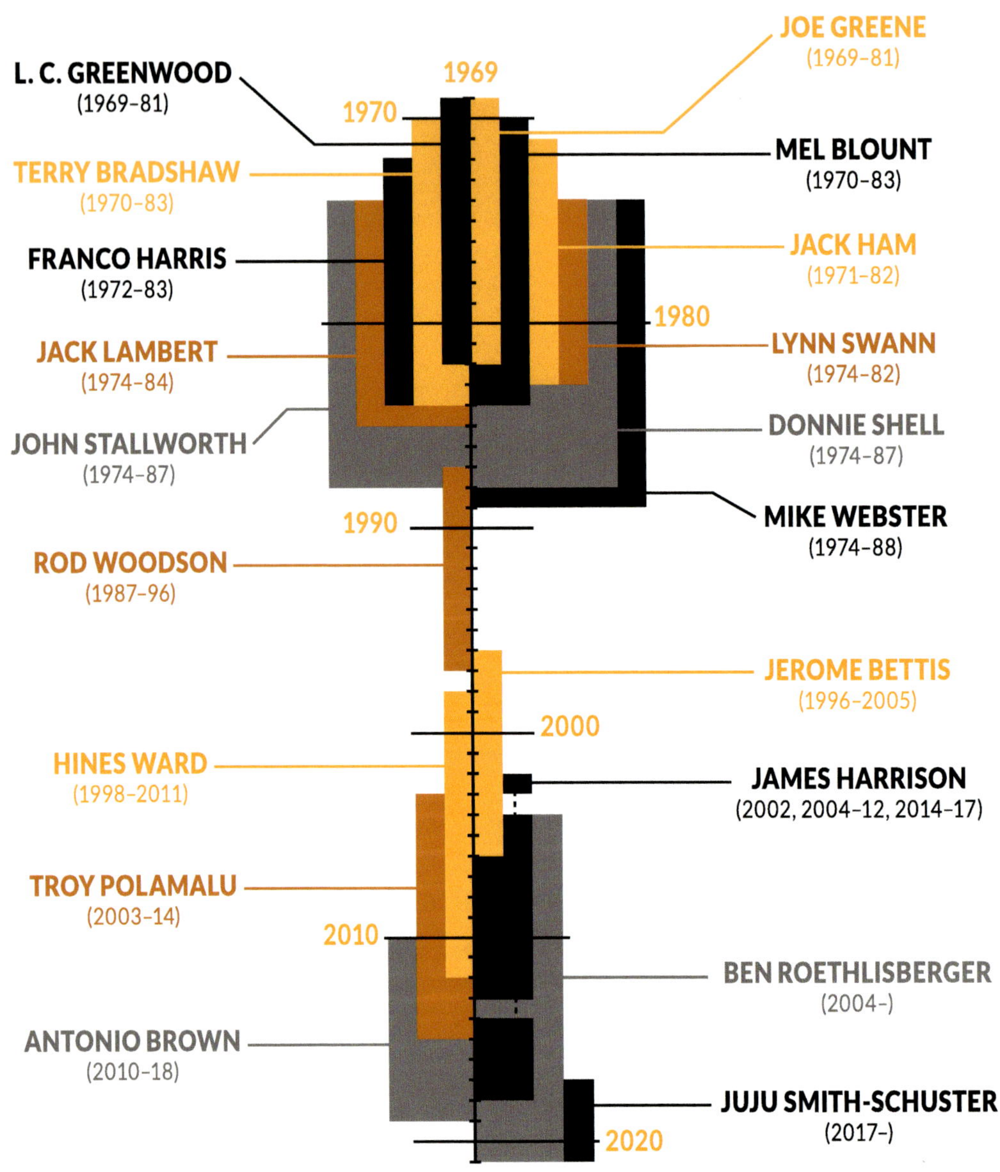

TEAM FACTS

PITTSBURGH STEELERS

Founded: 1933 (as the Pittsburgh Pirates)

Other names: Phil-Pitt "Steagles" (1943), Card-Pitt (1944)

Super Bowl titles: 6 (1974, 1975, 1978, 1979, 2005, 2008)*

Key coaches:

Chuck Noll (1969–91), 193–148–1, 4 Super Bowl titles

Bill Cowher (1992–2006), 149–90–1, 1 Super Bowl title

Mike Tomlin (2007–), 145–78–1, 1 Super Bowl title

MORE INFORMATION

To learn more about the Pittsburgh Steelers, go to **pressboxbooks.com/AllAccess.**

These links are routinely monitored and updated to provide the most current information available.

**1966 through 2020*

GLOSSARY

cornerback
A defensive player who covers wide receivers near the sidelines.

draft
An event that allows teams to choose new players coming into the league.

linebacker
A player who lines up behind the defensive linemen and in front of the defensive backs.

Pro Bowl
The NFL's all-star game, in which the league's best players compete.

sack
A tackle of the quarterback behind the line of scrimmage.

secondary
The defensive players who typically cover wide receivers.

INDEX